GALAXY OF SUPERSTARS

Ben Affleck

Backstreet Boys

Garth Brooks

Mariah Carey

Cameron Diaz

Leonardo DiCaprio

Tom Hanks

Hanson

Jennifer Love Hewitt

Lauryn Hill

Ewan McGregor

Mike Myers

'N Sync

LeAnn Rimes

Britney Spears

Spice Girls

Jonathan Taylor Thomas

Venus Williams

CHELSEA HOUSE PUBLISHERS

GALAXY OF SUPERSTARS

Ben Affleck

Sam Wellman

CHELSEA HOUSE PUBLISHERS
Philadelphia

Frontis: *Wearing a beard for his role in the highly acclaimed* Shakespeare in Love, *27-year-old Ben Affleck has made it to the top as one of the film industry's hottest young actors.*

Produced by
21st Century Publishing and Communications, Inc.
New York, New York
http://www.21cpc.com

CHELSEA HOUSE PUBLISHERS

Editor in Chief: Stephen Reginald
Managing Editor: James D. Gallagher
Production Manager: Pamela Loos
Art Director: Sara Davis
Director of Photography: Judy L. Hasday
Senior Production Editor: LeeAnne Gelletly
Publishing Coordinator: James McAvoy
Contributing Editor: Anne Hill
Cover Designer: Terry Mallon

Front Cover Photo: AP/Wide World Photos TOUCHSTONE PICTURES
Back Cover Photo: Photofest

The Chelsea House World Wide Web address is
http://www.chelseahouse.com   JB A257we

First Printing

1 3 5 7 9 8 6 4 2

Library of Congress Cataloging-in-Publication Data

Wellman, Sam.
  Ben Affleck / Sam Wellman.
  64 p. cm.—(Galaxy of superstars)
  Includes bibliographical references and index.
  Summary: A biography of the film actor who, with his longtime friend Matt
Damon, received the 1998 Academy Award for Best Original Screenplay.
  ISBN 0-7910-5231-1 (hc) — ISBN 0-7910-5331-8 (pbk.)
  1. Affleck, Ben, 1972–   —Juvenile literature. 2. Motion picture actors and
actresses—United States—Biography—Juvenile literature. [1. Affleck, Ben, 1972– .
2. Actors and actresses.] I. Title. II. Series.
PN2287.A435W45   1999
791.43'028'092—dc21
[b]   99—23594
                                                          CIP
                                                           AC

Contents

1

WORDS OF GOLD

In the spring of 1997 in Cambridge, Massachusetts, a movie crew hustled to set up a scene while veteran actor Robin Williams waited for the call to action. Behind the lights and cameras, two young men also waited and watched. Bystanders might not have recognized the 24-year-old Ben Affleck. At 6' 3", he was broad shouldered and lean. His neat brown hair topped a long handsome face whose expression remained cool and almost serene as his dark-brown eyes took in the scene around him. Beside Ben stood another not so well-known figure, his buddy Matt Damon, 26, stocky, and blond. Matt's face flushed pink with excitement.

A voice boomed, "Let's roll camera. Sound. Speed. Scene forty-one, take one. Marker. Action."

Good Will Hunting was filming it's very first take, or scene. Robin Williams began speaking his lines. Ben and Matt blinked at each other as tears streamed down their cheeks. This seemed to be the most wonderful moment of their lives. Then the take was over, and Williams spotted

---

Ben Affleck and Matt Damon astonished the film world with their screenplay for the movie Good Will Hunting, *and Hollywood honored them for their words of gold. An elated Ben, clutching their Oscar, hugs Matt Damon after the young duo won the 1998 Academy Award for Best Original Screenplay.*

The script of Good Will Hunting *appealed greatly to veteran actor and star Robin Williams, who was willing to take a supporting role to be in the film. With nothing but praise for Ben and Matt, Williams, well-known for injecting his own lines into films, played it straight, respecting the writers' words.*

Ben and Matt. Noticing how emotional they seemed, he walked over to them and gently placed his hands on their shoulders. "It's not a fluke," said Robin. "You guys did it."

Ben and Matt were in awe of the famous actor, and his praise thrilled them. They were even more thrilled when, to their astonishment, everyone on the set burst into applause. The ovation was for them: Ben Affleck and Matt Damon had coauthored the script for the film. Williams commented on that emotional scene: "[Ben and Matt] had this dream a long time ago and it was finally happening. It's a lot to take in."

As filming continued, Ben and Matt were more than spectators on the set. Both young men also played major roles in *Good Will Hunting*. Matt took the starring role of Will Hunting, while Ben played Chuckie, Will's friend. They even wrangled parts for their good friend Cole Hauser and for Ben's younger brother, Casey. For the two writers and actors, helping to create and being a part of the film was a magical experience. Ben played his scenes beautifully. And Robin Williams, who is known for improvising by injecting his own lines, was respectful of their script, which pleased Ben and Matt even more.

Williams was blunt about it. "The truth is, the thing is so good it didn't need me to improvise. The writing was so strong it doesn't need anything. . . . There's an emotional core to *Good Will Hunting* that came from Ben and Matt. They have this unspoken twins thing. They care for each other." Ben jokes about it, "We don't fight. We just pout."

"Ben and I were pinching ourselves every day," said Matt, the more serious of the two. "This had been such a long road for us and to look over and see your best buddy on the set every day is just an amazing feeling. . . . Also to watch his work . . . he's just a tremendous actor. He's the best young actor in the world, I think, for my money. Without a doubt."

When Ben was asked why his role in the film was much smaller than Matt's, Ben answered, "When you see the movie from the outside you think 'This is the main guy and this is the supporting guy.' But it was such a collaborative

As Chuckie and Will, Ben (left) and Matt ponder their lives in a scene from Good Will Hunting. *Although Matt took the leading part, Ben found his lesser role immensely gratifying. For the first time as a young actor, he had a serious, meaningful role.*

effort that it doesn't bother me. I just wanted to do interesting stuff and stop . . . slamming high school kids up against lockers."

Ben was referring to all the low-budget movies he had made in which he played a high-school jerk. He and Matt had written *Good Will Hunting* for the very purpose of giving themselves meaningful roles and showing that they could be serious actors. The effort had taken them five years. "This film was many, many years of work," said Ben. "Whether it's success-ful or fails, I want to take the victory lap now, just to say, 'Hey, at least we did it: we wrote it, we set it up, we did what we wanted to.' It's a movie I'm proud of."

Robin Williams echoed Ben's pride. "I'm very proud of this movie. It has a resonance."

After completing *Good Will Hunting,* Ben and Matt hurried off to other acting jobs. Ben took a role in the blockbuster *Armageddon,* starring Bruce Willis. Matt was cast in the title role in Steven Spielberg's *Saving Private Ryan,* a World War II film that would be a major hit.

As the movie industry began to speculate that *Good Will Hunting* might become a significant film, Ben and Matt were interviewed by reporters from *The New York Times Magazine, Gentleman's Quarterly,* and *Esquire.* One public relations man commented that because other reporters read these magazines, anyone they covered became a "buzz," a much talked about hot newcomer. Before long, Ben and Matt were buzzes, and reporters were eager to interview the pair. Still, all the hype was not about to phase the two friends. "'[B]uzz' in the end is worthless," said Ben realistically.

In Hollywood, acceptance at the box office is all-important, and a film's success is judged by the number of tickets it sells and dollars it earns. Everyone involved in *Good Will Hunting* was anticipating its opening. When it finally premiered in Los Angeles in December 1997, Ben and Matt experienced their first real taste of fan frenzy. Ben took it all in stride and appeared quite cool, whereas Matt was visibly shaken. Fortunately for Matt, everyone relaxed at the postpremiere party. Much to the delight of Ben and Matt, and in keeping with both their Boston backgrounds and the setting of the film, New England clam chowder and Boston cream pie were served. When he was asked how he felt about the premiere and the reaction of the theater audience, an elated Ben replied, "People just seem to like the movie and we just feel like we kind of won the lottery."

Ben was anxious about the critics' response, however. He need not have been, for the film was highly praised. Although *Good Will Hunting* opened in only seven theaters, it drew large crowds, and it appeared the film was going to attract a huge audience when it opened nation-wide. However, neither actor was prepared for what happened next. Matt was nominated for an Academy Award for Best Actor, the film industry's highest award for achievement as an actor. Instead of being honored, Matt was embarrassed. "The biggest sadness I have is that I look at my role in *Good Will Hunting* and I think that Ben could easily have played it. I think he let me do it because literally, he's my best friend in the world and he's that selfless."

"We're not competitive," insisted Ben. "We've always rooted for each other and I think that's the key to a successful friendship. You can't be too competitive."

Ben had plenty to be happy about anyway. The young duo won the 1998 Golden Globe Award for Best Screenplay and topped that by being nominated for an Academy Award for Best Original Screenplay, beating out such notables as Woody Allen. Moreover, Ben was dating actress Gwyneth Paltrow, another young "buzz," and was being treated like a real movie star. Everyone knew that *Good Will Hunting* was a box-office smash, sure to take in more than $100 million. An Oscar for Ben would really be the icing on the cake. Matt agreed, bubbling,

"Oh, boy. No, man, it's too much. Definitely too much. I can't even comprehend this."

The Oscars ceremony, held in Los Angeles on Monday evening, March 23, 1998, was nerve-wracking. As usual, the nominees sat in full view of television cameras, anxiously waiting to hear the winners announced. Despite the pressure, Ben was excited. Sitting among veteran film stars, he felt as if he had been time warped into a roomful of his heroes. Whatever happened, no one could take this great joy from him.

Sitting next to their mothers, whom Ben and Matt had escorted to the ceremony, the pair waited as the evening progressed and others stepped to the stage to receive awards. Among them was Robin Williams, who took home the Oscar statuette for Best Actor in a Supporting Role for *Good Will Hunting.* Although Matt was edged out as Best Actor by Jack Nicholson for *As Good As It Gets*, the two friends could still garner an Oscar for their screenplay. The moment was finally at hand, and when their names were announced as winners, they could not believe their ears. An Oscar! Ben and Matt seemed to catapult onto the stage, both flashing grins a mile wide.

Ben did most of the speechmaking, which included an incredibly modest thank-you. "We're just two young guys who were fortunate enough to be involved with a lot of great people."

2

GROWING UP IN THE BOSTON AREA

Benjamin Geza Affleck was born on August 15, 1972, in Berkeley, California, to parents of Scotch-Irish ancestry. Ben's middle name honors a Hungarian friend of the family. Before brother Casey was born three years later, the Afflecks moved all the way from the West Coast to the East Coast to live in Cambridge, Massachusetts, a suburb north of Boston.

Ben's first clear memories were of Cambridge, where he teethed not so much on Boston's famous baked beans and codfish as on the exploits of the Red Sox baseball team and the Celtics basketball team. The great Red Sox hero of his youth was the ageless Carl "Yaz" Yastrzemski. Nothing captured the hearts of self-confident Bostonians, however, as did their basketball team, the cocky Celtics. Ben was seven when 6'10" Larry Bird arrived in 1979. Bird, who first impressed Bostonians as a "country bumpkin," revealed himself to be a magician with a basketball. He also had an attitude. "I'm here. Who wants second place?" echoed Bird's playground imitators, flipping passes

The bridges and church steeples of Boston were familiar to Ben and Matt. Both grew up about two blocks from each other in the Boston suburb of Cambridge, home of Harvard University and the Massachusetts Institute of Technology. They drew on their knowledge of the area for Good Will Hunting *to show the different worlds of Cambridge and the working-class neighborhood of South Boston.*

blindly behind their heads or rainbowing three-point shots.

Most Americans know about the Boston area's unique history, including the ride of Paul Revere and the exploits of the Boston Tea Party during the American Revolution. They may not be that familiar, however, with Boston's history of attracting immigrants. First came the Puritans from England in the 1600s, the people who founded the city of Boston. In the mid-19th century, driven by famine and persecution in their homeland, Irish immigrants flocked to South Boston. In the late-19th century, Italians migrated into North Boston. Later, African Americans populated the inner city.

Cambridge itself is a college town, boasting not only Harvard University and the Massachusetts Institute of Technology (MIT) but the women's colleges Wellesley and Radcliffe as well. Students and faculty in the area colleges number more than 30,000.

Recently Matt explained that both he and Ben "grew up in Central Square, which is kind of between Harvard and MIT . . . in a multicultural neighborhood that was working class."

It was inevitable that Ben and Matt Damon would become friends. The boys not only lived a mere two blocks apart on Pearl Street and attended the same elementary school, but both boys' parents were very active in local theater groups. Some amateur actors in the Boston area even got a shot at Hollywood. Many movies and television shows filmed on the East Coast are cast in the Boston area. If nothing else, a youth with the ambition to act might appear as an extra in a crowd scene.

Both Ben and Matt aspired to become actors and became involved in performing at an early age. When Ben was only seven years old he got his first break, being cast, without credit, in *The Dark End of the Street*, a gritty film about life in South Boston. Getting the role was no fluke. He was a clear-eyed, clean-cut, all-American boy, totally relaxed and at ease in front of the camera. Matt's professional career got off to an early start as well when he began working in children's theater groups at about the age of eight.

While buddy Matt, like many actors, began by acting in plays on the stage, Ben began his acting career in front of the camera. Following his first film, Ben was picked to play C. T. Granville, host of the PBS television series *The Voyage of the Mimi*. The series was filmed over several years, with the first voyage of 13 quarter-hour episodes about scientists studying whales. The second voyage was 12 episodes that chronicled archae-ologists' search for a lost Mayan city.

Years later Ben recalled, "Acting for me was more like 'You know, I really kind of like this. This is fun.' It was just something that was really pleasant and when you're young, it's about being comfortable." From Ben's view-point he was just a normal kid who got lucky and was having a good time. Matt saw it differ-ently, however. "Ben was like the biggest star in Cambridge, Massachusetts, and he was *my* best friend. I was the theater kid and he was the television kid."

Although Matt was two years older, he respected Ben, who became his mentor for act-ing in films. Everything about film acting has to be understated: makeup, voice projection, and gestures. Movie people loved to tell stories about Hollywood legend Gary Cooper, best known for his films *Sergeant York*, *Pride of the*

Yankees, and *High Noon.* Actors and directors trained in the theater were at first disgusted by Cooper's style: "[O]n the set you'd swear it's the worst job of acting in the history of motion pictures," related director Sam Wood. "[Yet] on the screen, he's perfect."

Gary Cooper was considered the master of film acting, completely dominating every scene with the slightest gestures. He performed not for an audience sitting off in the distance but for the cameras, which magnify an actor's smallest expressions. Ben learned this and other techniques as well. When addressing viewers, Ben learned to never look into the camera. In a scene with another actor, he knew he must always look into the actor's eye closest to the camera. If he glanced from eye to eye, he would give the effect of "ping-pong" eyes darting back and forth.

Ben knew the stories of how famous actors had manufactured their trademark characteristics. Big John Wayne intentionally walked pigeon-toed and stiff-legged to get his trademark "head-long walk." Tiny but tough Jimmy Cagney dangled his arms not at his sides but slightly in front of his body—with his hands turned unnaturally sideways. These "attention getters" were for superstars, however, not for the likes of a young actor like Ben. Besides, these tricks would be considered scene stealing.

Although Ben starred in an educational series, he didn't enjoy watching these kinds of movies—nor did he like artistic films. Ben told *Gentleman's Quarterly,* "I am not a kid who was weaned on Fellini." He was referring to Italian director Federico Fellini who was known for his visual artistry and life-probing films.

Instead, Ben loved the blockbuster fantasy films Hollywood was beginning to produce in

Even when he was a child actor, Ben dreamed of appearing in fantasy blockbusters. His dream finally came true many years later when he starred in the action-packed box-office smash Armageddon. *Here Ben is in a publicity photo from this science-fiction adventure film, in which he plays a scrappy oil-rig worker contracted to save the doomed earth from an asteroid that is hurling toward it.*

the 1970s. The delightfully horrifying *Jaws* of 1975 and its spinoffs, *Jaws II* and *Jaws III*, were among his favorites. Ben wondered what could be more fun than playing Luke Skywalker in *Star Wars* or its sequels, *The Empire Strikes Back* and *Return of the Jedi*? Ben felt he was in heaven when he lounged in the Summerville Multiplex engrossed in *Star Wars*, *Raiders of the Lost Ark*, and other fantasy movies. "*Back to the Future* was the best film I saw that year," he insisted later of the 1985 blockbuster.

But Ben did not spend all his time at the movies or making them. He and Matt went to

Ben has always been very close to his mother, Chris, here with Ben (at left) and Matt and his mother, Nancy, at the 1998 Academy Awards. Chris raised Ben and his brother on a schoolteacher's salary when father Timothy left the family.

public school and led relatively normal child-hoods. They buddied around with other boys, played Little League, threw their share of snow-balls, rapped as "Matty D and Bizz," gloried in the pelting rain, and suffered summer sun-burns. Nevertheless, they were not average kids. Ben was a minor celebrity around Cambridge. Matt was also well-known, not only because he acted in local theater groups but because he also had an unusual home life. He and older brother Kyle lived with their divorced mother, Nancy Carlsson-Paige, a professor of early childhood education, in a three-story gray colonial house with five other families. Ben visited the communal house so often that many housemates thought he lived there too.

Ben did not think the arrangement seemed unusual, as he explained: "You say commune and you start to think of some off-in-the-wilderness, barefoot, and bell-bottoms, sort of flaky hippie living. But this was a much more practical arrangement." Matt had to laugh. "Actually, you could call them hippies. They had all the same views on money and politics, raising children. My mom is a very radical lady."

One of Nancy's most radical acts was making Matt cook. Later Ben remembered, "My mom was trying to get me to do more work around the house and would say, 'Well, Matt's mom makes him cook once a week.'" Ben joked, "So I first knew him as a guy who was really setting a bad precedent in the neighborhood."

Ben's mother, Chris, taught elementary school and tried very hard to create a normal home environment for Ben and his brother, Casey. She enforced discipline but also enjoyed bantering with her two wisecracking sons. The family had problems, however. Ben's father, Timothy, tried his hand at acting and then writing while also tending bar and working as an auto mechanic. Unfortunately, he began drinking, and eventually the Afflecks' home life became stormy. Finally, when Ben was 12 his father left the family. "I was kind of relieved," Ben admitted years later.

Meanwhile, Ben palled around with Matt, attended drama classes at the Cambridge Rindge and Latin High School, and continued to make movies.

3

MAKING MOVIES

Young Ben Affleck suspected that scores of people had to be involved in creating one of his beloved blockbusters. After all, he was amazed by the number of people who worked to film a modest series like *The Voyage of the Mimi*. Those whom viewers see on the screen—the cast of actors—are only a small part of the effort.

It takes an entire team to make a film. Whoever backs a film with money is the producer, who can choose to be active in the filming or may go virtually unseen. Usually the driving force behind a movie, and the one who has the overall concept of a film, is the director. He or she consults with the screenwriter, closely directs the actors, and manages all the activity of the technicians on the set. Matt Damon would say years later, "Movies . . . need a strong voice and a decisive voice and the director is that voice."

A set can be outdoors on a particular location or inside a building on a soundstage. The cinematographer is in charge of the cameras and lighting. The appearance of the set is the responsibility of the art director, who is helped

---

Scores of people are involved as a camera crew prepares for a location shot. Although Ben had begun his acting career when he was only seven years old, he was not really aware of the incredible number of jobs and people involved in making films. But he was eager to find out as he pursued his acting in television films.

mainly by the set designer. The gaffer is the chief electrician, the grip is an all-purpose helper, like a stagehand, and the prop keeps track of all of the properties or items needed on the set. Other important crew members bear the self-explanatory titles of sound recorder, makeup, costumes, set decorator, special effects, stunts, and camera crew.

Ben learned quickly that making a film was a total group effort and that everyone on the set became almost like a family. In fact, many actors feel more at home on a set than anywhere else, bonding to all the other members of the cast and crew. All work hard in a common purpose: to create a fine film.

There are others besides those on the set who are also involved in filmmaking as well. Without a good script by a screenwriter, actors can flounder badly. And written records must be kept of every scene filmed, which is the job of the continuity clerk. An editor is one of the most important off-set people on a film. He or she, usually working with the director, takes all the scenes and puts them together to help bring continuity to the drama and action of the film. The final product can be quite different from what the actors and director envisioned. Actors can find that some of their scenes have landed on the "cutting-room floor." Some might even find their characters cut out completely. It is a common complaint among actors that editing has changed their superb film into a disaster.

Almost all productions have music, called a score, which is added for mood and background. The composer is the person in charge of creating film music. Matt once sat in on recording a movie score. "It was like this sixty-five piece orchestra. It was unbelievable. The music just comes right at you, washes over you."

Before the production can even begin, however, readers sift through screenplays sent to the producer by hopeful writers. When a promising screenplay is chosen, a casting director has to search out actors for the various roles. Often the director auditions actors for roles. Many films require a second unit, a crew that films scenes, often on location, that don't require the presence of the director. After the final product is assembled, publicists promote the film to the public in various ways. If the film is intended for movie theaters, a very important part of the venture is distributing the film.

Having gained a great deal of this film knowledge, Ben Affleck passed on his know-how to buddy Matt. "Of course I thought he knew everything because he'd done the PBS show," Matt said later. In fact, Ben did know a great deal and not just from playing in *The Voyage of the Mimi*. At 14, he was cast as Danny in the ABC-TV after-school special *Wanted: The Perfect Guy*, a film about a boy trying to find the perfect mate for his mother. Ben was enthusiastic at his first opportunity to act with a well-known professional, Madeline Kahn, the Boston-born actress best known for her parts in Mel Brooks's wild comedies such as *Blazing Saddles* and *Young Frankenstein*. Kahn had also distinguished herself playing Ryan O'Neal's girlfriend in the highly acclaimed *Paper Moon* in 1973.

Ben hoped that this opportunity would help push him into real Hollywood films. His dream did not seem beyond his reach, although many child actors do not fare well as they mature. Their failure to secure stardom as adult actors has destroyed some lives, as they often turn to alcohol or drugs. Ben, however, seemed unaware of the potential pitfalls as he took Matt under his wing.

"[W]hen he was fourteen and I was sixteen," recalled Matt, "[Ben] came up to me, in his infinite wisdom . . . and said, 'I can get you an audition.'" The two boys were allowed to go to New York City, where Ben introduced Matt to his agent. While Matt never got an audition from the encounter, Ben continued to get parts.

In 1987, at the age of 15, Ben got the role of Billy Hearn in the television detective movie *Hands of a Stranger*. The director was Larry Elikann, who had once directed Michael J. Fox, star of *Back to the Future*. Ben was thrilled to be working with the film's stars, Armand Assante and Blair Brown, both highly regarded actors. As the jobs kept coming in, both boys' mothers worried about the ambitions of their kids. Ben explained, "I think our parents were concerned because everybody knows that acting is a difficult career. I don't think they were happy with the prospect of their kids facing a lifetime of rejection and scraping."

Ben threw himself into high-school life, studying acting under the tutelage of Jerry Speca, a bushy-browed, mustached man who was an outstanding drama teacher. For Ben's first couple of years of high school Matt was also in Speca's acting group. This group won praise for many of its productions from Boston's leading newspaper, *The Boston Globe.*

Ben continued to pursue acting outside of school as well. Years later, discussing his acting

Besides appearing in a number of television films, Ben also studied acting. At an early age he learned how to use his eyes and facial expressions to convey emotions, one of the many important talents necessary for film actors who must play up close for the cameras. Expressive by nature, Ben did not find this task difficult.

as a youth, he said, "I worked here and there in Boston and shuttled down to New York, and I'd do TV movies, episodics and so forth. . . . My mother never wanted me to be a child actor who's, like . . . into the world of kid actors and stuff. So, I would always stay in school and maybe do something in the summer for a couple of weeks."

At 16, Ben landed his first leading role in a movie. The film was about Eskimos, and with this experience Ben learned a bitter lesson about filmmaking. Describing his disappointment some years later, he remembered:

> They ended up shutting down and firing everyone . . . I was really heartbroken. It was called Atuk. . . . [So] I figured out the business could be kind of a letdown, early on. . . . Professional acting is such a tenuous game, so flighty and fickle. You can feel like a pro one minute and be unemployed the next.

Still, Ben and Matt talked about acting all the time. The pair deliberately picked the less popular one of the two cafeterias in their school so that no one would disturb them as they discussed their plans to become actors. "It was kind of nerdy, actually," Ben later admitted.

It appeared to be an odd friendship since Ben, although younger, seemed the older of the two. Matt almost always deferred to Ben as if he were an older brother. Ben even drove the car, a brown 1977 Toyota Corolla station wagon he bought with $400 of his acting money. Matt had not accumulated enough to buy a car. Their differences also appeared in their personalities. Matt was much more outgoing than Ben, and he felt completely comfortable with girls, whereas Ben did not. Although both young men were highly intelligent, it was Matt who pulled down top grades, and Ben who was the classic underachiever. They even teased each other about this difference. Ben dubbed Matt the "warrior" and Matt called Ben the "clown."

For a long time, Ben did not realize how this difference in their academic outlooks would send them off in different directions. When Matt graduated from high school, he left for prestigious Harvard University. Having many

questions about the wisdom of pursuing a career in acting, he chose to be an English major. By now both knew that only a handful of actors ever made a lot of money in their profession. Most actors were poorly paid, if they found work at all. At any time 85 percent of the more than 20,000 actors who belong to the Actors' Equity Association are unemployed. Despite what could be a gloomy prospect and sad to see his buddy leave to pursue a new life, Ben was determined to be a working actor at all costs.

From their childhood days, when they first met, both Ben and Matt (right) had a common interest. Both loved acting. They talked about it endlessly and supported each other's ambitions, sometimes going separate ways but always pursuing their goals.

4

APPEARING ON
THE SILVER SCREEN

"I started high school five foot one and hairless," Ben once joked. At 15, in a Burger King commercial, Ben was a mop-topped kid so undersized he could barely see over the dashboard of a car. In his junior year in high school, however, he zoomed up to 6' 3". "My knees and shins and elbows would just ache every morning," he said.

But Ben's record growing spurt did not vault him onto the school's basketball team. He remained a self-professed acting "nerd." He also studied as little as possible, ushered at the local multiplex, visited Matt at nearby Harvard, and indulged his passion for acting under Jerry Speca. "He taught kids self-discipline, how to take responsibility for themselves," Ben later said of his first acting coach.

Under Speca's direction, Ben discovered that performing on the stage was quite different from acting in films. He saw stage actors' exaggerated voices and gestures as overstated, and playacting seemed unnatural to him. The actor was also playing to a live but distant audience, not an all-magnifying camera. Ben did, however, enjoy one difference between stage and film acting. Because a play is a continuous process he could build a character as the

---

Hollywood, California, is the mecca for young actors who hope to become film stars. Ben had honed his acting skills and learned all he could about moviemaking when he took off for the capital of the film world with a single ambition—to make his mark on the silver screen.

plot progressed. If he chose to, he could even portray the character differently in different performances.

There was little about acting that Ben did not study. He learned the ancient art of basic storytelling, the first element of which is the quick introduction of a conflict or a problem. Then the struggle to overcome the conflict must be skillfully portrayed. Of course the plot is strewn with additional obstacles to overcome. Last of all is the relatively quick resolution of the conflict. This simple scheme of storytelling is the basis of most films and stage plays.

Despite what he was learning, youthful Ben did not quite appreciate the difficulty of the craft he was trying to master. Unlike the stage, film scenes are not necessarily shot in the same order as they occur in a story. Consequently, a film actor has to be extremely disciplined, having a grasp of the total character so that he or she can pluck out just the right emotion at any given time. Moreover, if a scene has to be filmed more than once—which is often the case—an actor has to repeat emotions without losing believability. The closeness of the camera is merciless at detecting the smallest flicker of insincerity on an actor's face.

During the last two years of high school Ben felt that he had accumulated the skills necessary to be a good actor. Unfortunately, this realization alone did not secure acting jobs. He began to suspect Matt had made the right choice by going on to Harvard and more opportunities. Almost in a daze, Ben graduated from high school and, with no better plan, followed his girlfriend to the University of Vermont, where he continued his career as an uninspired student.

Finally in 1991 at the age of 18, he gave up

college in the east and headed for Los Angeles, California. He would go to college there, he thought, but always in the back of his mind was acting. He enrolled at Occidental College as a Middle Eastern Studies major. His only connection to the Middle East was the fact that he adored the classic 1962 movie *Lawrence of Arabia*. Ben did have a real connection in California, however. His father, Timothy, was there, finally working out his problems with addiction in a rehabilitation center. Later, Ben would say that one of the great moments in his life was his "father checking himself into rehab in 1990. I was very pleased and enormously relieved." The two soon reconciled.

The academic rigor of college was not for Ben, however, and he soon dropped out to make the rounds auditioning. Ironically it was Matt, still the Harvard student, who had gotten a part in a

Ben was a great fan of Peter O'Toole, seen here in his starring role in one of Ben's favorite epics, Lawrence of Arabia. *Ben would later appear in a film with O'Toole, but first, the aspiring young actor had to make his own mark in the movies.*

television movie. Called *Rising Son*, it starred Brian Dennehy and Piper Laurie. When it aired in the summer of 1990, critics praised Matt for his acting skills.

Ben was not without luck of his own. In October 1991, viewers could catch him in a television film adaptation of the Danielle Steele book *Daddy*, starring Patrick Duffy and Lynda Carter. Ben got the juicy role of a rebellious 18-year-old who fathers a child and leaves high school. He appeared in more than two dozen scenes, several of which were highly charged with emotion. In his big scene, which was several minutes long, he pleaded before a judge for custody of his baby. Although the film demonstrated that Ben was a serious actor with real range, there were no immediate follow-up offers for other good parts.

In the meantime, Matt had made a choice that would bring the two friends together in a Hollywood film. Two semesters short of gradua-tion Matt dropped out of Harvard to pursue an acting career. Ben and Matt were both cast in the 1992 film *School Ties*, a story about anti-Semitism in a prep school, which was being shot in the Boston area. Matt got the substantial role of a bigoted, wealthy youth while Ben was cast in a lesser role as another well-to-do preppie.

Once the cast was assembled and Ben saw who else was included, he was discouraged about ever being discovered as a screen actor. Besides Ben and Matt, many other talented and good-looking young actors appeared, including Brendan Fraser, Chris O'Donnell, Cole Hauser, Andrew Lowery, Randall Batni-koff, and Anthony Rapp. And these were just a handful of the ones starting out. The lead roles in other big films were being snapped up by

Ben got his first break on the big screen with his role in School Ties. *In this publicity shot for the film, Ben appears in a sullen pose in the right background, with Chris O'Donnell standing above him and Matt lounging in front on the steps. Ben was not happy with his role of a rude, bigoted preppie and began to get discouraged about his prospects in acting.*

young stars who had already arrived, such as Tom Cruise, Johnny Depp, Denzel Washington, and Brad Pitt. "By the time Matt and I . . . [got] a script, 18 other people had to have passed on it," grumbled Ben.

It seemed to Ben that he would never get a break. In *School Ties*, Brendan, Matt, and others had roles far more significant than his. Fraser as hero and Matt as villain were especially lucky because their roles were pivotal to the plot. Although Ben was on camera a lot, his lines were minimal. In a dining room scene he joked about the busboy, and in a classroom scene he hardly spoke more than a dozen words of dialogue. To make it worse, Ben's character was unlikeable, selfish, and sarcastic. *School Ties* hardly showcased the young actor's charisma.

However, some positive elements grew out of Ben's experience with *School Ties*. Both critics and moviegoers liked the film, and Ben liked the serious theme of prejudicial injustice against Jews. He was also glad that Matt was singled out for praise. In addition, Ben made a lot of friends among the up-and-coming actors, especially hitting it off with Cole Hauser.

Although Chris O'Donnell's role in *School Ties* was small, Ben watched as Chris suddenly became a star. Chris landed choice parts in two hit films, *Scent of a Woman* with Oscar-winner Al Pacino, and *Fried Green Tomatoes* with Oscar-winner Kathy Bates. Matt spoke for Ben as well as himself when he said, "A lot of people got hot off that movie [*School Ties*], but I wasn't one of them . . . . Chris O'Donnell got to be huge out of that movie and I'd be lying if I said there hadn't been some envy there."

Ben and Matt could not know it at the time, but an idea they had for a film would make them as huge as O'Donnell. The friends had become enthusiastic about a film script that had grown out of a one-act play Matt had written for a playwriting class while still at Harvard. He had invited Ben to join him in the fun of performing the play at Harvard under the critical eyes of the faculty. The two friends acted out the script, trying to improve it, but the effort was unsuccessful. Matt had developed interesting characters, but the plot fizzled out.

Matt recalled what followed later: "[I]n March of 1993, I went to Los Angeles for an audition and while there, showed it to Ben again. . . . He liked it but didn't know where to go with it either. But it was then that we made a pact that we would work on it together."

In the beginning the two buddies had no thoughts of writing a film script. They merely enjoyed the intellectual exercise. It was like old times in the high-school cafeteria when the pair blocked out the rest of the world and just talked acting.

Following *School Ties*, Ben and Matt went their separate ways. Matt got a significant part in the 1993 film *Geronimo: An American Legend*. Ben too was appearing on the screen, usually in films produced by independent filmmakers outside the big Hollywood studios. His first effort was in 1993 with his appearance in an offbeat comedy, *Dazed and Confused*, a nostalgia movie about suburban high-school kids in the 1970s. The film got good reviews, but Ben was not happy with his part, because even though he had more dialogue, he again played a kid with a cruel streak. That same year, Ben added to his television credits when he was cast in a dramatic series called *Against the Grain*. He was sure that this was going to be his ticket to fame.

5

SCREENWRITER

In *Against the Grain*, Ben, now 21, played 16-year-old Joe Willie Clemons, a high-school quarterback whose new coach was his own father. Despite Ben's high hopes, the series did not take off. The fate of a television series is determined by how many people watch the show, and *Against the Grain* did not attract a large audience. By the end of 1993 the series had been canceled, and once again Ben was looking for work. "Ben would be in a series, like eight episodes," shrugged Matt later.

Matt himself wound up no better off than Ben following his role in *Geronimo*. Despite a superb cast that included Robert Duvall and Gene Hackman, and a gorgeous setting, the film was burdened with a weak storyline. It was a flop with both critics and moviegoers. Instead of being part of a blockbuster, Matt was part of a disaster. He had spent three months shooting in the desert, rising before dawn, spending days thirsty and chap-lipped. The experience did not deter Matt from pursuing an acting career, however, and he set out for California to join Ben.

Ben in the television series Against the Grain *with costar John Terry. This series seemed like the chance for Ben to really shine as an actor and get away from roles he referred to as unlikeable jerks. When the series flopped, he and Matt decided to become screenwriters as well as actors, beginning their five-year struggle to get their script for* Good Will Hunting *to the screen.*

Sharing a cramped apartment in Los Angeles, the lifelong best friends did what they could to get by, accepting parts in some very forgettable films. It was here they decided to write their now-famous screenplay and give themselves the starring roles that were eluding them.

In 1994, the two young hopefuls, along with another friend, were sharing a rundown apartment in the Eagle Rock area of north Los Angeles. With Matt there, living accommodations were a little tight, and Ben had to sprawl out on a couch. With what seemed like little or no prospects of getting starring roles, Ben and Matt returned to their project of working on the script. "I didn't have a job and things weren't looking too good for me, so why not?" remembered Ben. Focusing on their script, called

Good Will Hunting, the duo decided to expand the earlier play into a screenplay for a film. Why couldn't they sell the screenplay to a movie studio and write in starring roles for themselves? Sylvester Stallone had done that very thing in 1976 with *Rocky*. Although Ben and Matt did not dream they could make a blockbuster like *Rocky*, they hoped to create an intelligent movie to highlight both their acting and writing talents to the industry. "We originally wanted a movie that was a show-case," said Ben later.

With the bad luck they were having at being discovered, they now needed their film script more than ever. As they wrote, the characters began to develop. They would play wisecracking tough guys from the working-class neighbor-hood of South Boston. The hero would be Will Hunting, a mathematical genius, played by Matt. Ben would be Will's best friend, Chuckie.

Because Ben typed faster, he was usually at the keyboard. As both of them fired off dialogue, Ben hammered out line after line, page after page. They found it was easy, almost like the bantering they had indulged in with each other for years. Neither felt as if he could write one page of script unless the other was there to bounce the ideas back. Separately they wrote nothing, but together they were creating an incredible screenplay and treasuring every word they wrote. Soon their script was more than 1,000 pages. "We had 'Will Goes To The Zoo episodes!'" they joked later.

In the midst of their writing, they still audi-tioned for parts and also moved from apart-ment to apartment, always trying to get closer to the film industry centered in the southwest part of Los Angeles. Despite the lure of being young and single in the big city, Ben and Matt seldom partied, instead devoting their free time to working on the movie script.

Finally by November 1994 they had shortened *Good Will Hunting* to a realistic length. Matt begged his agent to shop it around to the various studios. His agent agreed, even though Matt and Ben made his chore harder by insisting they had to get the roles of Will and Chuckie. "It was a given we would star in our own movie," Matt said later.

On November 13 one studio offered them $15,000 for the script. Ben and Matt would have jumped at the offer, just to assure themselves the film would be made with starring roles for themselves. But Matt's agent urged them to be patient. Then lightning struck. For four days various studios continuously bid against one another for the script. Ben and Matt felt like they were in paradise. Executives at Castle Rock liked the script so much they offered the writers a staggering $600,000, but with conditions. The wild story, in which Will Hunting discovers a monstrous scheme of the FBI and the space agency NASA had to be rewritten. "Stick to writing real people and don't trick it up with all this other stuff," said the executives at Castle Rock.

Ben and Matt accepted the offer and began revising their script, changing it from a thriller to a character study. Meanwhile, they pursued their respective acting careers. In 1995 and 1996 Ben acted in two low-budget independent films. In *Mallrats* he once again played the cruel jerk. His only progress was that he now played an older jerk. In *Glory Daze* his task was to make Jack, a sarcastic, cynical, disrespectful college man, a likeable character. It didn't work.

When, at the end of the film, Jack's parents leave in exasperation, most moviegoers could well understand their decision.

Ben did play one commendable character when he appeared in an episode of the HBO television series *Lifestories: Families in Crisis.* His work in the 30-minute episode, "A Body To Die For: The Aaron Henry Story," earned him an Emmy nomination, television's award for excellence. Even though Ben did not win, he was glad to continue revising *Good Will Hunting* with Matt.

Working as long and hard as they could, Ben and Matt soon toned down their story. The screenplay no longer involved an evil scheme by the FBI and NASA. Will became a young janitor at the Massachusetts Institute of Technology, an undiscovered mathematical genius who defies authority so recklessly he seems headed for prison. His genius is redirected, however, when he comes under the guidance of a sensitive psychologist. Pleased with the revisions, Castle Rock made plans to go ahead with the movie.

There was one obstacle, however. Ben and Matt protested about the location of filming. "[W]here it was going to be shot was really, really important," Matt explained later. Castle Rock wanted to film in Canada, where it is much cheaper to make movies. Because *Good Will Hunting* had become a real labor of love for Ben and Matt, they insisted that their story had to be filmed in their beloved Boston area. Angry Castle Rock executives agreed to let Ben and Matt shop the script around to other studios if they paid Castle Rock what had already been spent developing the film.

Now Ben and Matt had to get an offer of

In revising their screen-play for Good Will Hunting, *the duo gave Matt a love interest, played by Minnie Driver, here with the two writers. Her role added spark to the film and to Matt's love life, when they became a Hollywood couple.*

$1 million for the script to be able to pay back the studio! To make their task even more difficult, the script was no longer a thriller but a drama— a much riskier venture in the eyes of most movie studios. Moreover, Ben and Matt were now rumored to be hard to work with. Then came a real mountain to climb—a dead-line. If Ben and Matt could not sell the script in 30 days, Castle Rock was going to go ahead with production. Ben later remembered, "I was told if we couldn't get another offer for the script, we'd be lucky to get tickets to the premiere."

Worse still, if Castle Rock retained the rights, Matt and Ben would not get the roles of

Will and Chuckie. What a gamble the two buddies were taking now! As each of the 30 days
passed, the task seemed more and more
impossible. Finally only three days remained.
In desperation Ben took the script to Kevin
Smith, his director in *Mallrats*. Ben begged him
to read it, and Smith reluctantly agreed. Ben
waited anxiously. This had to work. Ben and
Matt had exhausted all other possibilities.

6

THE BIG TIME

"I absolutely loved it," gushed Kevin Smith of the script for *Good Will Hunting*. "Within two days," said Matt, "the deal had been made and we were at Miramax." Smith had taken the script directly to the top executives at Miramax Studio. They loved it too—enough to pay Castle Rock $1 million to take it off their hands.

Weeks later, Ben's life seemed truly miraculous when Miramax told him that Mel Gibson wanted to be in *Good Will Hunting*. Gibson, the hottest star around, had produced, directed, and starred in *Braveheart*, which had just won the 1995 Oscar for the Best Picture of the Year. As it turned out, however, Gibson had conflicting commitments, and the deal fell apart. Once again, the film stalled as Miramax waited for just the right combination of ingredients before starting production.

While *Good Will Hunting* languished, Ben was cast in *Going All the Way*, another nostalgia film set in the early 1950s. His role as Gunner Casselman, a returning Korean

---

When Ben and Matt ran into some roadblocks that delayed the filming of their screenplay, Ben took a lead role in the film Going All the Way. *Although critics did not like the film, Ben found portraying a returning Korean War veteran a gratifying serious role. The film also brought him to the attention of several industry executives who considered him a potential leading man.*

War veteran, was a great improvement over the roles he had been playing. He also liked the subplot that told how the war erased Gunner's prejudices. Although the film starred well-known actresses Jill Clayburgh and Leslie Ann Warren, critics did not like the R-rated film. With the film being based on the novel by Dan Wakefield, they had expected more from it. Critic Leonard Maltin's acidic comment was that the movie, set in 1954, "opens with a huge 1957 pop hit—never a good sign."

There was one good sign, however. Critics noted that Ben had the qualities of a leading man. "Affleck reveals a hunky, leading-man quality," wrote one reviewer. Ben had made a breakthrough. At least some people in the film industry saw he had true potential. Ben's next effort came in *Chasing Amy*, in which he had the lead role of comic-book artist Holden McNeil. Critics liked the film and Ben's performance, but like so many other low-budget independent films, *Chasing Amy* did not attract a large audience.

Then Ben snagged another role with an independent company shooting Dean Koontz's science-fiction thriller *Phantoms*. Heading the cast was Peter O'Toole, the charismatic star of the desert epic *Lawrence of Arabia*, one of Ben's all-time favorites. O'Toole had matched histrionic fireworks with acting legends such as Katherine Hepburn and Richard Burton. And his career credits spanned *Lawrence of Arabia*, 1962's Best Picture of the Year, to *The Last Emperor*, the Best Picture of the Year in 1987. Ben relished working with and talking to the legendary actor of the silver screen.

On one occasion, noting the frigid location

for their shooting, Ben commented breezily, "I would rather be in the Saudi Arabian desert." O'Toole froze Ben with his ice-blue eyes. "No, you wouldn't," he said grimly, completely blowing Ben away.

Shooting the film was like paradise for Ben. Was he really sitting around bantering with Peter O'Toole? The only drawback to *Phantoms* was that its release was going to be delayed many months. Unfortunately, contrary to his high hopes, Ben and *Good Will Hunting* would not get an immediate boost from the release of *Phantoms*.

Ben works with director and writer Kevin Smith on the set of Chasing Amy. *Smith, who was instrumental in getting Ben and Matt's screenplay to Miramax studios, wrote the part in* Chasing Amy *specifically for Ben.*

Huddled together with Peter O'Toole (wearing a sweater), Ben and other cast members play a scene in the thriller Phantoms. *Although Ben did not have a leading role, he was awed at working with the legendary O'Toole.*

Meanwhile, Matt got a break that, in turn, did help their film. In the summer of 1996, he landed the lead role in *The Rainmaker*, directed by Hollywood heavyweight Francis Ford Coppola. The film is an adaptation of one of John Grisham's best-selling novels. The story revolves around a young lawyer who takes on a large and unscrupulous insurance company that consistently bullies people and systemati-cally denies proper compensation for legitimate claims made by desperate victims. "The day after I got *Rainmaker*, I sent [Miramax] a fax," Matt later bubbled, hoping to prompt a reaction.

His ploy worked. With Coppola's reputation as a director and Grisham's popularity as a novelist, Miramax immediately realized that *The Rainmaker* could be a huge hit and wanted to ride its tailwind. The studio was now committed to releasing *Good Will Hunting* in theaters shortly after *The Rainmaker* came out in order to take advantage of Matt's rising popularity. At last Miramax was prepared to launch an all-out effort. First they hired Gus Van Sant to direct the movie, but they needed a star to play the psychologist, Sean McGuire.

Van Sant approached Robin Williams, the rubber-faced comedian who was also a major dramatic star with successes including *Dead Poets Society* and *Good Morning, Vietnam*. Williams would certainly attract large audiences, but he had to be convinced of the talent of these two young newcomers before signing on with the project. "When are your fathers getting here?" quipped Williams on meeting the two fresh-faced youths. Matt and Ben's writing spoke for itself, however. "I just read this extraordinary script and said, 'I have to be part of this,'" Williams later related.

Ben began to wonder just how big their movie might be. He admitted that before Robin Williams joined the cast, "We never thought anyone would see it."

As casting progressed, Ben's younger brother, Casey, was asked to play a character named Morgan, and good friend Cole Hauser was cast as Billy. Along with Ben and Matt, the guys portrayed cruising "southies," working-class young men from South Boston.

The film was not created overnight and Ben and Matt continued to polish the script while acting in other films. They experimented with more plot developments, such as having Will or Chuckie die. It soon became apparent, however, that new plot twists were not necessary. The script was solid, especially after they added a love interest for Will Hunting, a college coed named Skylar. Matt read lines with Minnie Driver when she auditioned for the part. He later commented, "She starts and I totally blank. After four and a half years of trying to get this movie made, I didn't know where I was, who I was, or what was going on." There was little doubt that Minnie Driver was perfect for the part and she won the role as Matt's love interest.

At long last, the crew and cast gathered in the Boston area to shoot *Good Will Hunting.* Swedish actor Stellan Skarsgard had been selected to play the math professor who discovers Will's genius. The five main characters were now set: Ben, Matt, Minnie, Stellan, and of course Robin Williams.

From the start, Williams amazed Ben and Matt. As if flicking off a light switch, Williams was able to completely subdue his wild, off-the-wall comedy. Matt said later: "It holds Robin back being the funniest man in the world. People really don't give him the credit he deserves as an actor. I think a lot of people think of him as this funny man who channels, where he's actually this person who works extraordinarily hard. Robin is very serious and intense in this role and that's how he was when the camera was rolling. But once the camera cut, he was the Robin

Williams you see all the time, running around the room doing his stuff and making everybody laugh."

After weeks of shooting, the cast and crew held a wrap party to celebrate the end of filming. Not only had shooting been fast and flawless, the product seemed almost perfect. Everyone involved had made a fine film, and it became obvious that *Good Will Hunting* was going to shape the rest of Ben's life. Word spread among the studios that the film might be a huge success, and Ben was flooded with offers. He was now a red-hot property.

7

MOVIE SUPERSTAR

After the success of *Good Will Hunting*, Ben achieved another cherished goal. At last he would take a leading role in a major summer blockbuster. Touchstone Pictures cast Ben as oil-well worker A. J. Frost in *Armageddon*, a science-fiction thriller. The film's star, Bruce Willis, leads a team of drilling specialists, including A. J., into space to intercept and blow up a meteorite headed for earth. At NASA's rocket-launching complex in Florida, one of several locations for the lavishly budgeted movie, Ben rested in luxury between takes. His personal trailer was enormous and plush, an extravagance that made Ben uncomfortable at first.

"[I]t was difficult for me to adjust. I felt intimidated by the scope of the movie, and by the company I was keeping." Emoting in a blockbuster was different too, but he adjusted. "Once I figured out that I had to draw a little more broadly to compete with the kind of histrionics and cacophony that were going on, it became easy."

With his role in the action-packed Armageddon, *Ben, here with Bruce Willis, was finally on the road to superstardom. Because Ben was known to many of his fans for his good work in independent films, he was criticized for "selling out" to commercial interests. Ben has replied by saying, "I take it that they're conferring some kind of integrity on me . . ." and by pointing out that he has always loved blockbuster movies.*

After 24 days of shooting *Armageddon*, Ben said, "[O]n an independent film we would be done by now. On *Armageddon* we probably shot a minute and half of screen time. I didn't say a line all week. And I have a big part. . . . You think of action films as frenetic and crazy, and it's actually much more boring."

An action film is the ultimate challenge to an actor intent on remaining in control of the character he is playing. The movie was filmed in bits and pieces over a period of many weeks in several locations and not in chronological order. Ben took advantage of the idle time, however. He took his visiting mother on side trips, including a trip to the Everglades, where they skimmed across the swamps in an airboat. The headiness of fame has not diminished Ben's closeness to his mother and the two still lovingly trade wisecracks at a lightening clip.

Ben escorted his mother to the 1998 Academy Awards ceremonies, but he took girlfriend Gwyneth Paltrow to all the parties afterwards. For a dozen years Ben had dated Cheyenne Rothman, an old flame from Cambridge. That changed when he met Gwyneth, a long-necked blond beauty who also acted in some films for Miramax. Ben's father even knew Gwyneth's mother, veteran actress Blythe Danner. Gwyneth herself was a very busy thespian, acting in 12 films in just four years. In 1996 she blossomed into a leading actress in *Emma*. One of Gwyneth's best friends was actress Winona Ryder. After an introduction, Matt, fresh from a breakup with costar Minnie Driver, and Winona became a couple too, and the foursome often double-dated. No one was at all surprised that these young, emerging film stars were strongly attracted to one anther.

While he seemed head over heels in love, as far as his career was concerned Ben tried to keep his feet on the ground. "You can't assume anything in this business. There are a lot of examples of people who got launched in huge movies and just disappeared."

Somehow this seemed unlikely for Ben. He was too serious, talented, and hardworking, with a contract to do more films for Miramax plus the freedom to take other roles too. Ben began making movies at a feverish pace. In 1998 he played Bartleby in Kevin Smith's

Ben shares in the trophies awarded by the Screen Actors Guild to cast members of Shakespeare in Love. *Next to him are Gwyneth Paltrow, Geoffrey Rush, and Ruppert Everett.*

Dogma, a controversial yet satirical fantasy about angels, which also starred Matt. In *200 Cigarettes*, with his brother, Casey, and Courtney Love, Ben portrayed a bartender. He also took a small role in *Shakespeare in Love* so he could spend time on location in England with Gwyneth, who was the film's star.

The two resisted all prying into their relationship. "All I'll say is he is very bright and very funny," Gwyneth said to a reporter.

About England however, Ben was effusive in an interview:

> It was actually kind of nice to come here because it was much more relaxed. I shot this movie [*Dogma*] in Pittsburgh . . . and I wasn't used to that sort of level of people knowing who I was. It sort of made me uncomfortable to be honest with you, but here it has been much more relaxed, or much more at ease. I don't know if they know who I am but they have played it really cool.

When *Armageddon* was released in July of 1998, Ben became a frequent guest on television talk shows. He projected intelligence, good humor, and fashion sense, often sporting a charcoal gray business suit, white shirt, muted gray tie, and black dress shoes.

Ben got good reviews for his performance in *Shakespeare in Love* after its release in late 1998, and he would soon add a second Oscar-winning film to his list of credits. *Shakespeare in Love* was nominated for 13 Oscars and won seven, including Best Picture of the Year and the Best Actress nod for Gwyneth Paltrow, who thanked Ben in her acceptance speech.

Early 1999 saw the release of *200 Cigarettes*, followed by *Forces of Nature*, in which

Ben survives a hurricane and a plane wreck while attempting to join his fiancée. Along the way, sparks fly when he meets an attractive free spirit played by Sandra Bullock.

Ben's life off-screen was also dramatic. In late 1998, Ben and Gwyneth split. The two young stars with skyrocketing film careers found it difficult to maintain a relationship. They have remained friends, however, even joking about their breakup when Gwyneth

One of Ben's costars has commented that "Big Ben is one of the funniest guys I've ever been around." He proved it when he played opposite Sandra Bullock, here with Ben in a scene from Forces of Nature.

hosted *Saturday Night Live,* an event that provoked Hollywood gossip about a renewed relationship.

Ben has many future films planned, some in production, such as *Reindeer Games* and *The Third Wheel,* and some only proposed, such as *Desert Blue, Like a Rock,* and *Balling the Jack.* He has not forgotten his collaboration with buddy Matt. The duo began creating another script for a film entitled *Half Way House.* To create the script, Ben drew on his father's experiences with alcohol addiction and his success as a counselor with other recovering alcoholics. Once again the pair retained choice roles for themselves, with only one difference: this time Ben will be the star.

CHRONOLOGY

1972   Benjamin Geza Affleck is born on August 15 in Berkeley, California.

1973   The Affleck family moves to Cambridge, Massachusetts.

1980   Meets best friend Matt Damon; discovered for PBS series *The Voyage of the Mimi*, which is filmed over several years.

1984   Family splits up when father leaves for California.

1986–87 Appears in television films *Wanted: The Perfect Guy* and *Hands of a Stranger.*

1990   Graduates from high school; briefly attends University of Vermont.

1991   Moves to California, enrolls at Occidental College, and continues auditioning for film roles.

1992   Cast in *School Ties*, his first role on the big screen.

1993   Matt moves in with Ben in California; begins cowriting screenplay for *Good Will Hunting* with Matt; appears in *Dazed and Confused*; stars in TV series *Against the Grain.*

1994   Ben and Matt sell *Good Will Hunting* to Miramax.

1995–96 Appears in *Mallrats* and *Glory Daze*; stars in "A Body to Die For: The Aaron Henry Story," an episode of the HBO-TV series *Life Stories: Families in Crisis* and earns Emmy nomination.

1997   Appears in *Going All The Way* and *Chasing Amy*; films *Good Will Hunting.*

1998   Wins Oscar with Matt for Best Original Screenplay for *Good Will Hunting*; stars in *Armageddon*; appears in *Shakespeare in Love*; films *Dogma.*

1999   Appears in *200 Cigarettes*; stars in *Forces of Nature*; films *The Boiler Room* and *Reindeer Games*; writes *Halfway House* with Matt; named to *Premiere* magazine's list of the 100 Most Powerful People in Hollywood.

FILMOGRAPHY

Television

1984	*The Voyage of the Mimi* (series)
1986	*Wanted: The Perfect Guy*
1987	*Hands of a Stranger*
1991	*Daddy*
1993	*Against the Grain* (series)
1995	"A Body to Die For: The Aaron Henry Story" (HBO series special)

Films

1992	*School Ties*
1993	*Dazed and Confused*
1995	*Mallrats*
1996	*Glory Daze*
1997	*Going All the Way; Chasing Amy; Good Will Hunting*
1998	*Phantoms; Armageddon; Shakespeare in Love*
1999	*200 Cigarettes; Forces of Nature, Dogma*

AWARDS

1995–96	Emmy nomination for "A Body to Die For: The Aaron Henry Story."
1997	Academy Award for Best Original Screenplay (cowinner with Matt Damon) for *Good Will Hunting*.

FURTHER READING

Altman, Sheryl. *Matt Damon and Ben Affleck: On and Off Screen*. New York: HarperCollins/HarperActive, 1998.

Engel, Joel. *Screenwriters on Screenwriting: The Best in the Business Discuss Their Craft*. New York: Hyperion, 1995.

Freely, John. *Blue Guide to Boston and Cambridge*. New York: W. W. Norton, 1994.

Maltin, Leonard, editor. *Leonard Maltin's 1999 Movie & Video Guide*. New York: Plume (Penguin), 1998.

Mayfield, Katherine. *Acting A to Z: The Young Person's Guide to a Stage or Screen Career*. New York: Watson-Guptill, 1998.

Straczynski, J. Michael. *The Complete Book of Screenwriting*. Cincinnati, OH: Writer's Digest Books, 1996.

Tracy, Kathleen. *Matt Damon*. New York: St. Martin's Paperbacks, 1998.

ABOUT THE AUTHOR

SAM WELLMAN lives in Kansas. He has degrees from colleges in the Midwest and from Ivy League colleges. Wellman has written a number of biographies for both adults and young readers, including subjects as diverse as *George Washington Carver*, *Mother Teresa*, *Billy Graham*, and *Michelle Kwan*.

INDEX